This book belongs to:

Rudy Brass

Published by Ladybird Books Ltd
A Penguin Company
Penguin Books Ltd, 80 Strand, London WC2R 0RL, UK
Penguin Books Australia Ltd, Camberwell, Victoria, Australia
Penguin Books (NZ) Ltd, Cnr Airbourne and Rosedale Roads, Albany, Auckland, 1310, New Zealand

1 3 5 7 9 10 8 6 4 2

© LADYBIRD BOOKS MMIV

Printed in Italy

The Body

written by Lorraine Horsley
illustrated by Gustavo Mazali

The body is working all the time.
Here are some parts of the body you can see working.

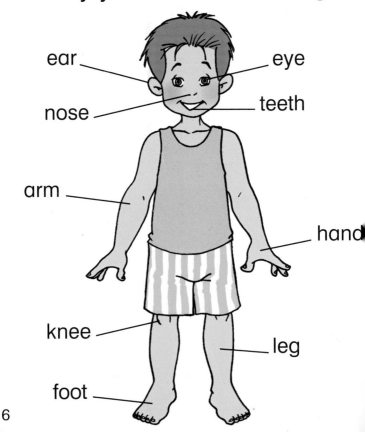

ear

eye

nose

teeth

arm

hand

knee

leg

foot

Here are some parts of the
body working inside you.

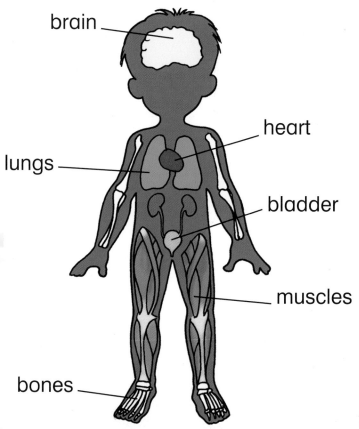

brain

heart

lungs

bladder

muscles

bones

When I eat, my teeth help me to chew my food and my tongue helps me to swallow it.

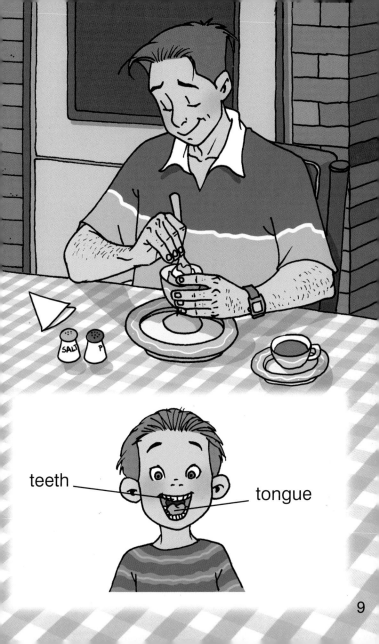

teeth

tongue

When I walk, muscles pull on my bones to make my legs move.

An adult has 639 muscles in their body.

leg bone

leg muscle

When I am in class, my ears help me to hear and my brain helps me to think.

We hear when sound waves vibrate on the eardrum inside our ears.

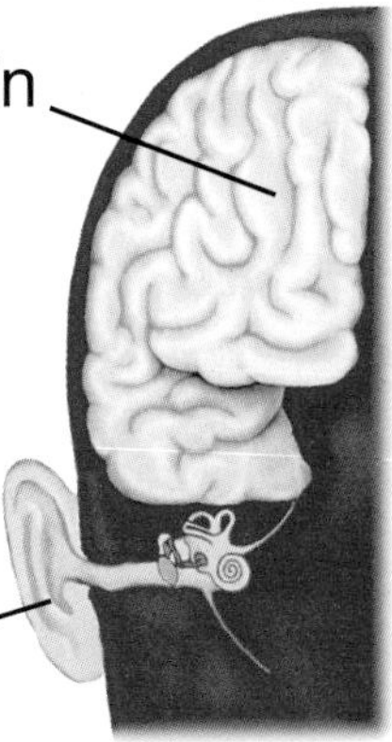

brain

outer ear

When I am playing basketball
my eyes help me to see the
ball and my brain tells me
to move.

We see when
light passes
through the eye
and sends a
signal to the
brain.

brain

eye

When I run, I breathe faster.
When I breathe, my lungs
take in oxygen.

Your lungs breathe in and out 22000 times every day.

lungs

When I exercise, my heart beats faster. My heart pumps blood all around my body. The blood takes food and oxygen to my muscles.

Exercise is good for your heart and it makes your muscles grow stronger.

heart

When I am hot, my skin goes red and it starts to sweat.

When sweat
dries on your
skin, it cools
you down.

sweat

skin

21

When I go to the toilet,
my body gets rid of
liquid and waste.

When you drink,
liquid passes
through your body
and leaves your
bladder as urine.

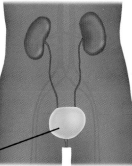

bladder

When I fall over, my knee starts to bleed. The blood makes a scab to stop me bleeding.

New skin grows
under the scab.
Then the scab
falls off.

scab

new skin

When I sleep, my body rests and grows.
My body is working all the time.

An adult needs to sleep for seven or eight hours every day. A baby needs to sleep for 18 or 20 hours.

Can you remember parts
of the body you can see
working?

Can you remember parts of the body working inside you?

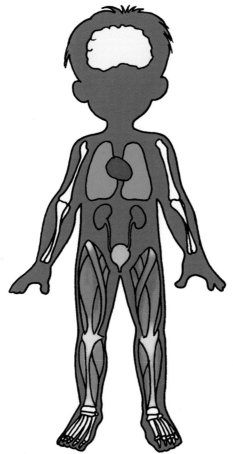

Index